CSU Poetry Series LIX

The Largest Possible Life

poems by Alison Luterman

For Phillip,
Waltzing with you
is a dream.
Thanks for your
all your support.
Love,
Ali

Cleveland State University Poetry Center

Acknowledgments

"The Dog Next Door," "Insomnia," "Being Alone," "Angel Rant," "Driving Through Heavy Fog," "Invisible Work," "Listening to Helen Caldicott on the Car Radio," "Ode to the Jacuzzi at the 23rd St. Y," "Swaying Slightly in Geoff's Hammock," "Accidents," "The Notary Public," "Jesus Incognito," "Stripping," "Moss Landing," "Morning in the Mission; Grandpop Comes to Visit," "Stolen Sentences for Abraham," "City Beach," "Interlude," "Full Moon," and "The Night Crawlers" were all published in *The Sun*.

"I interview sex workers and write down what they say" was published in *Kshanti*.

"Janus" was published in *Slipstream*.

"On Not Flying to Hawaii" was published in *Home Planet News*.

"Fairy Tale" was published in *Poetry East* and *Poets and Artists of the Northwest Calendar*, 1996.

"The Justice of the Peace" was published in *The Billee Murray Denny Anthology*, 1994 and *A More Perfect Union: Poems and Stories about the Modern Wedding*, eds. Esstman and Hartman.

"The Largest Possible Life" was published in *Storming the Gates: An Anthology of Women Writing about Spirituality*.

"Valentine's Day in the Eighth Grade" was published in the *California Poets in the Schools Anthology*, 1998.

"Blood Rant" and "Outdoor Wedding" were published in *Poetry East*.

"Monogamy" and "The Man in the Dogtooth Leggings" were published in *Whetstone*.

The Ohio Arts Council helped fund this program with state tax dollars to encourage economic growth, educational excellence and cultural enrichment for all Ohioans.

The Largest Possible Life

Special Thanks

Thank you to the gentle and generous Sy Safransky, editor of *The Sun*, who extended a continuing yes. The women of Sixteen Rivers Press, Valerie Berry, Margaret Kaufman, Jackie Kudler, Diane Lutovich & especially my Sunday writer's group, Terry Ehret , Nina Lindsay, Carolyn Miller & Susan Sibbett, critiqued & enthused over these poems with fierce & loving attention.

Thank you to my parents, David & Cari, my brothers & sisters: Dan, Emily, Jim, Patti, Vicky, David & Sairey, and my nephews, Joshua, Noah, Branden, Jarid, Theo & Eli, for being the roots & branches of my tree. (And to cousins, aunts, uncles & grandparents.) Thank you Alan Sagan for showing me how infinite love is. Thank you Arlene Sagan, fellow-artist-mother-in-law. Thank you Chuck Ries for being catalyst, muse, & goad. Thank you everyone in Queer Minyan and Pardes Rimonim (and in my greater Jewish communities) for spiritual sustenance and kvelling.

California Poets in the Schools offered the chance for employment(!) as a poet, and sharing with other teaching poets whose friendships I treasure. Thanks also to the teachers & students whose classrooms I visited. Thank you to Joaquin Miller Park for being a beauty place I could always go to walk, and to Alameda Beach for tidal wisdom and joy. To Helen Graham Cohen & family, my first best friend & home away from home always.

To Bill Corbett, early mentor, for opening my mind on long walks all over Boston. Thank you Ted & Suzanne Hinman for enduring love, to Jeremy & Vicky & all the other VISTAs who were in Miami with me '81-82, for tears, laughter & survival. Thank you Boston Theater Group for love & Shakespeare, & Anna Warrock for stone soup poetry. To the La Pena Community Chorus for song & fellowship.

Thanks Bob Fitch, for taking me canoeing, for singing, dancing & loving. Thanks to Tim Perkis for cutting the CD. *Gracias a Oscar Zavala por su amistad.* Thank you Blake Aarens for truth, inspiration and love. To members of the Bay Area Country Dance Society for spinning me around. Thank you, Michael Parrish, dharma brother, for soul companionship, & to Susan Wooldridge for initiating me into the inner guide meditation.

Thanks to Marianne Regan for skillful listening, to Lisa Moss for walks around the lake, to Lisa Klein & the other actors of DolphinTales theater group for serious play, to Carla & Mike Zilber-Smith for mutual dedication to art. Thank you to all members, past and present of Cactus Rose collective, & to Patty and Abraham & the other neighborhood children for shameless beauty & unquenchable love.

Last but not least, thank you very much Bruce Weigl, for selecting this manuscript, for your generous encouragement, and for your time. Thank you to Ted Lardner at the CSU Poetry Center for help in preparing the book, and to Lauren Dana Kline-Ari for her magnificent illustrations. And to Ruth Schwartz, for *being* love, in so many myriad forms, my God, if I thanked you adequately, I would never ever stop.

This book is dedicated to:

Ruth L. Schwartz

Emily Jane Koester

and Patty Kenard

Table of Contents

III.

I

The Truth

I love the truth the way I love picking blackberries,
even as I'm scratched and burned and stung.
I love the tartness between my teeth and tongue,
feeling how old truths hung too long on a bramble go soft
    and cobwebby,
and truth picked too soon is full of acid.

It's what I love about writing, when I love writing.
How now and then, through the thicket of metaphor
you get a cool sweet berry of truth.
And even when what I want to hear is,
    I will love you forever,
    Your search has ended,
    You are the best! And
    You will be young and beautiful FOREVER!

The truth remains a sharp, nourishing comfort,

like these two old drunks, one black, one white, strolling
    arm in arm
up my street, commiserating:
"And I tell you I had alla them childrens!"
"Yep. That's how it was."
"*Alla* them childrens!"

I love how it hides itself like that,
between two plain green leaves,
and how much of it there is, like love,
yet never finished, never enough.

The Dog Next Door

How you love to write about God,
even if you don't know what to believe.
Especially because of that.

You love to write,
"God is speaking to us," or "God shows us,"
as if by writing you could make it so.

You're lonely,
and the pit bull next door is barking on his too-short chain.
You love to write, "Love is kept on a tight leash
in a concrete yard, barking and howling,"

and in this way connect your own pain
with that of the suffering animal
and the knotted up flow of love in the world,
as if invoking this way would solve something,

when what you really need to do
is call the S.P.C.A. , or better yet,
since you're a word person, find the words
to approach your neighbor: "About your dog?"

Still, you want to bring God into everything.
Mostly, you like the name,
the way it hangs like light around ordinary objects,
the grace it lends the least utensils.

There is some profound pleasure
in writing about simple things
that have been written about over and over
and letting God slip in between the lines,

while love, yes, alright, love
is kept on its too-short leash, barking and howling
and wind lashes the last of November's leaves
from the neighbor's yard into your own.

Insomnia

I am being cut into little pieces by the wind
and scattered over the city.
I am not snoring drunk under the overpass,
or huddled on a cot at the women's shelter, a black
eye giving away all my secrets.
I am not sleeping standing
on one leg like the heron
with the slicked-back Elvis haircut.
I am awake
like all the glimmering fish in the estuary,
swimming to unheard music,
through each   successive   eat-and-be-eaten
world:
Opal.   Emerald.   Ebony.

Awake like the fool
in the electric
blue business suit
who stands at the edge
of Lake Merritt
fishing
at 3 a.m.
in the heart
of the city.   He
grins to himself and casts his line
farther and farther out
as if he could hook the whole
glinting purple lake,
the clouds, the cars, the scudding night,
and reel it in, sing to it, and eat it.

Being alone,

I am never alone.
God supplies you in various disguises

scattered through my day like an overlooked miracle:
saint's face in an oil-slick puddle, say,

or the dog who comes up to investigate
and lingers an extra moment in communion,

or someone stooping to put arms around a crying child.
This is to counteract those mornings

when to wake is to face broken glass in the mirror
and the least touch shatters

everything; when I recall how you'd roll over, say Hello
Beautiful, smile, and lead me gently back

from the bad-dream labyrinth
into sunlight, hot sweet tea, and the next thing to do.

Now I muscle through fog alone,
on a different, meaner street, in an uglier time,

and there's a man who looks
like he's been shot out of a police siren

and spent too many nights trying to find his way home:
Hank. Always hangs around in front

of Max's Auto Detail — A Clean
Car is a Well-Running Car — lopes, half-bent

as if to straighten fully would hurt, yet
when I walk by with my red hair like a flag

from a country called Abandoned Woman and forty years
of disappointment showing

on my face, he never fails to gallantly rise
to the occasion and say "Hello Beautiful," and sometimes

"I seen you in your car yesterday."
As if he knew I were missing

some vital connection, something he could supply.
In just such small, exact details

God matches our need for each other
with our prayers for each other, to show us

if we pay attention, how the fabric of our long-lost love
can stretch to cover all the world.

Angel Rant

for Nehoma

I come into his room, the old junkie,
old alcoholic with obscene tattoos caressing the ropes of his
    biceps.
Four-thirty on a winter afternoon, early darkness,
I'm tired, don't want to hear any more wounds oozing their
    stories.
Still the soap operas spill
from every lighted room in this hospital.
And there's this guy,
his crooked inner arms hardened stiff from years of slamming
heroin into them. I say, "No problem,
we'll add it on so you won't have to get stuck again,
just sign if you want the test."
Pass the clipboard to him, his hands shaking so
I wonder how anyone will read it.
Scars and sores decorate the shipwreck of his face.

He tells me he killed a man once
when he was drunk. Says he believes
angels walk among us
because life isn't long enough to fix all our mistakes.
"I figure the most any of us is got is seven hundred months, give
    or take."
We talk about maybe getting off
drugs, booze, all of it. "I don't think I've got
another recovery left in me," he says.
His hair, thick horsetail curtains, is gray.
I look at his birthday number. He's almost to the end
of those seven hundred months.
"I tried and failed so many times, I think God's fed up with me."
"God doesn't get fed up, only humans. God's not
like that," I argue, hoping to believe it.
"Yes," he says, looking out the window

8

where the early evening angels are crowded,
their cheeks burning blue smoke, the winter angels.
And there are the black ones,
who ferry the body across the underground river,
and the golden angels of piss glinting in sunlight,
whose job is to announce
another ice-cold morning axed in half with hangover.
There are angels for this, yes, and they can be beautiful,
the heroin angels, when young,
their smiles glowing, and the melody of needles singing
inside their skin like a great swarm of enchanted bees.
Angels enough for everyone. I'm thinking how badly
we want what we want, all of us,
how we are still hoping for the angel
who will tell us what we need to know
in order to live, whether the word comes
in a squirrel darting across the hospital lawn or a dropped
     pigeon feather;
always, in the end, there's that glimpse of hope

we can't let go of—a child's sparkler,
bright, whirling, dangerous. It could burn you
if you reached for it directly. It could go out,
be swallowed in the open vault of blue-black heaven.
Oh, but the midnight skies are full
of other night-walkers carrying their tiny candles,
shielding them with a cupped hand the way a man
lying in a doorway will struggle to light a cigarette.
Any moment now, he may look up.

I interview sex workers and write down what they say

One had the name of her tribe
tattooed on her arm: "Urok,"
but she couldn't read it,
she couldn't read.

She was drunk
and far from home.

Weeping, she told me
she'd rather cut her throat
with the knife she carried in her boot
than work the streets again,

and when I foolishly said, "I understand,"
corrected me with great kindness:
"No, you don't,
and I hope you never will."

The Man in the Dogtooth Leggings

for Chuck, who heard it from Keone Nunez

You tell the story so I can see him,
the big Hawaiian guy covered with tattoos,
who danced hula, cried for a dead friend,
made his own pair of dog-tooth leggings.
How he traveled up and down the coast,
gray roads snaking like smoke
between the hips of mountains,
looking for roadkill, watching the horizon
for vultures.

He'd pull his old tin can of a car over
onto the shoulder of the road,
back up carefully
to greet an army of furious flies,
with only a bandana over his nose.
Most times it was squirrels,
raccoons, cats, once a deer—
not what he needed, so he'd drive on.

When it was a dog, a real dead dog lying there,
even half-eaten by maggots,
he'd get to work with a pair of pliers,
cold sweat prickling his neck,
the retch rising in his throat.
He'd pry open the stiff and stinking jaw
while his own gorge rose,
ignoring flies, worms, beetles, the cold glass eyes,
to get those teeth.

It is the only pair of real dogtooth leggings left
free in the world,

not locked like overlooked history in a museum somewhere.
That is why he had to make them himself.
He wears them to dance his survivor's story,
last remnant of a scattered and slaughtered tribe.

The stories we need are covered in flies,
smothered in death-stink.
They have been thrown out of car windows
at high speeds or hit head-on
when they tried to cross the highway.
Tourists doing 65 on their way to someplace else,
glimpse through glass
the man kneeling by the side of the road,
peer through blurred windows
at his painful retrieval of the almost-lost.

Blood Rant

(after Rilke)

Blood arranged in clear thin tubes like long-stemmed roses,
handled with latex gloves, evidence from an unsolved crime;
blood charged with invisible armies that swirl powerfully
    downstream,
the odor of edible flowers offered in the steam

of our fevers where a red cradle rusts
at the bottom of a crimson ocean
and it is the beginning once again — we must part
wave upon wave of torn wet flesh to get through

to the air. Blood of our nightmares:
bathed in blood, bloodlust, bloodthirst, bloodborne.
Our own blood we regard with horrified fascination and all
    our secret love.
Smelling of iron, of rust, of fresh, raw meat—

stink of the war-god's sweat-lodge,
smell of the birthroom, bathroom,
poems of protest scratched out with the bloody tip
of a broken finger. It is our life there,

bright red embarrassment, emblem of the vulnerable,
the brave and foolish sacrifice, blooming
out of us more honestly than words,
naked liquid flowers of the inner world...

The Four Horsemen Come to the Tenderloin

The end is coming
here in the Tenderloin
where you can buy whatever you want;
a kiss of white powder,
boys who look like girls,
girls who look like hell.

Here's the world's oldest living whore,
her face a weathered cave of ten-dollar blowjobs.

You can approach her, you know
and ask for anything,
anything at all.

And you can still get your morning coffee,
sweet brown dregs in a styrofoam cup
by the iron gates of Bodecker Park, —
"Soap Opera Park," they call it,
"Bull Dagger Park" —

It is not our fault
if the Apocalypse comes
while we are trying on shoes at the Goodwill.

       Sometimes
there's an irresistible urge
to lie down, right on the pavement,
like that fetal man who could be
either sleeping or weeping.

They won't kill you
if you can't pay your bills, will they?

The end is coming. No one

will notice it much. The four horsemen,
breathing fire, wild on crystal meth,
will dismount their hallucinatory horses and stand on line
with everyone else, waiting for soup at St. Anthony's.

The dream, meanwhile, goes on galloping.
The reins are out of our hands.

Driving Through Heavy Fog

The thought of death fills the rental car,
and you think, it wouldn't be so bad.
There's a dreaminess, a cushioning
of the night around you, deceptively soft,
as if to cross the divider over the line
into oncoming traffic would be to float, not smash —
as if to drift the other way
over the embankment
would be a slow-motion catapult
into another scene in the movie. Not an ending at all.

At least then I could stop
trying so hard,
you catch yourself thinking, your hands
a vise on the steering wheel,
eyes fixed on the dim flares of taillights in front of you,
the muscle in your neck
that wants to survive cramped
tight as a fist.

But then there's that other part of you
that's still so curious
that wants to know how your life will turn out.
Even knowing that it never turns out —
And that other one, the invisible child,
trustingly asleep in the back seat.
It's for her sake perhaps that you continue to struggle so valiant
to breathe, to roll down the windows and defog the windshield,
to stay awake tonight whether the stars care or not.

Invisible Work

Because no one could ever praise me enough,
because I don't mean these poems only
but the unseen
unbelievable effort it takes to live
the life that goes on between them,
I think all the time about invisible work.
About the young mother on Welfare
I interviewed years ago,
who said, "It's hard.
You bring him to the park,
run rings around yourself keeping him safe,
cut hot dogs into bite-sized pieces for dinner,
and there's no one
to say what a good job you're doing,
how you were patient and loving
for the thousandth time even though you had a headache."
And I, who am used to feeling sorry for myself
because I am lonely,
when all the while,
as the Chippewa poem says, I am being carried
by great winds across the sky,
thought of the invisible work that stitches up the world
    day and night,
the slow, unglamorous work of healing,
the way worms in the garden
tunnel ceaselessly so the earth can breathe
and bees ransack this world into being,
while owls and poets stalk shadows,
our loneliest labors under the moon.

There are mothers
for everything, and the sea
is a mother too,
whispering and whispering to us

long after we have stopped listening.
I stopped and let myself lean
a moment, against the blue
shoulder of the air. The work
of my heart
is the work of the world's heart.
There is no other art.

I went dancing while the bombs were falling

in Iraq, thousands of miles away.
While warplanes let loose
over a city of hungry people,
we in our meaty, exuberant American bodies
bounced together, glistening,
bopped up and down to the zig-zag guitars and scattershot drums,
gleaming with sweat and desire and misplaced rhythms.

Over there, veiled women, frantic to hide their children
got caught in a shower of fire
intended to take out a weapons lab. Some smart bombs went astray.
Some children whose bellies were torn open screamed all night.
Someone riding a bicycle back from the fields
had his arm and leg blown off.
At Barefoot Boogie, when we got hot, we shed some clothing
in our charming, casual American way. A man I didn't know
danced too close to me, his erection pressed against my leg.
Over there, they would have stoned us both for that.
Someone offered a prayer
for the American soldiers who were fighting "so we could dance."
Someone else muttered about cheap oil. We'd all driven cars
to gather here, on a cold winter night—
 "We didn't come for a political debate, let's boogie!"
A few faces still looked troubled.
But then the dee-jay put on "Born to be Wild"
and everyone shouted along.

Men!

I will name you so you no longer have power over me.

I will press my thumbs into the small of your back, into the muscles lining your thick thighs, your legs like tree trunks, your arms of meat and stone, your arms gone soft with helpless longing, your empty arms full of dream, your wiry dangerous arms, ready to wrestle, fight, hold off, your fingers full of the music of my wet, your searching, empty fingers.

I will enter your belly of war and hunch there among the smoke and bombs and terrified shouts of boys calling for their mothers. I will crawl along the darkness of your veins, tangling my hair in your black blood, leaning against the walls of your muscles, tracing my invisible code along the underside of your skin.

This is a spy mission. Drinking your scent like an animal, I go tracking a dark, secret, sour-smelling bulb or nut or essence, some bitter smell, armpits or groin, something in the tangled sweaty hair of you, skunklike but compelling. Some musk I want to eat. Above all, I want to feel my own slippery strength, wild in this impossible pursuit.

It's a lie. I want to eat your warrior's heart, your heart of splashed colors, your locked, private, rusted-shut, no-longer-edible heart, your heart of stalled cars and blind alleys, your woman's heart made of the same softness as my own.

I have crawled inside your ear. I am whispering down your nasal passages up the dry riverbeds of your ducts where a sharp gush of ebony tears are waiting to be wrung into my open hand. Don't worry, I will transmute everything into jewels, black pearls.

Ballad of Greg Withrow

Greg Withrow was a young neo-Nazi who organized the white
supremacist student movement in Sacramento in the 1980s. When
his first love affair caused him to spontaneously turn away from
hate, his own troops came after him.

1)
Love blindsided me.
Crept up in those dumb white
sneakers they make waitresses wear. This girl said,
"You seem like such a nice guy."
And she put eggs in front of me. I ate them,
though by then I was such a mess of mud inside
I couldn't hardly speak human.
Dirt with a pile of eggs in front of it.
Except she smiled or something.
So I went back. Went back for her smile
and her number. Love crept up
on dirt.

2)
She was new to town and didn't know.
She never seen the likes of what I was up to.
My job: big man on the hate rodeo.
Ride into town, get the white kids fired up
telling them how the niggers and spics
and jews had all the money, all the jobs.
Why they weren't getting any.
Under my direction a few black heads might get smashed
like pumpkins the day after Halloween,
or the body of some gook
show up in the tall weeds outside of town
with no one but his family to count him missing.
And them not even able to tell the cops in proper English.
I wanted to be like Hitler, or better, Genghis Khan.

3)
She didn't have family
neither. And my old man
used to like to
kick me downstairs from when I could walk,
until one night he kicked me out entirely.
On the streets, the Nazis was family, they took me in.
Because I was Aryan white, like them.
And we was going to someday rule again.

4)
What happened before doesn't matter.
What happened after I take as payment
on debts past due.
But I'll tell you something:
Love opens you up worse than a knife.
I've been stomped with steel-toed boots,
punched in the stomach, had my head swung into a wall,
into a toilet. Love is worse.
There's nothing to hold onto.

5)
See, we was family to each other.
She had no idea, she didn't know.
Little by little love was ruining me.
How could I eat her eggs and go out afterward
and preach kill the nigger? Kill?
I'd lift my head and it was another man,
a black man, eating his eggs
with maybe someone who loved him waiting at home
in their bed for him to make her warm.
And I couldn't do it. Love was ruining me.

6)
I tried to get away quiet.
Out by the back door. But Hate—
Hate really does not want to let you go
It thinks it owns you. And I owed
something, now. Would have to pay.
Still, when they came for me I was not ready.
Came with their baseball bats and smashed my jaw
so I couldn't talk to no more reporters,
and say that Hate thing was a mistake.
After, I wouldn't tell police who done it.
Hell, it was me who done it.
I trained me to come after me
in the middle of the night and leave me
in a pool of my own blood.
That's who done it.

7)
When I turned on her she left
and I don't blame her. I'd have drove her to the station
myself, if I knew what come next.
After the news that night when I kept on telling
the wrong I done and that I was sorry. They got me good—
nailed me to a six-foot piece of wood
like the savior of hell, and I come stumbling down the streets
    of Sacramento,
the nails in my hands, and blood
running down my side. And the white folks passed me by.
Like this I know God has a plan.
And nothing happens that He don't see.

8)
Cause my own Aryan Nation had warned me.
I was as good as dead already,
and the others they were afraid I think. My own people.
And then the black couple come.
And the man says "Is this who I think — ?"
And the woman says, "We got to take him down."
And the man says, "Hell, we got to, do you know who *this is?*"
And she says, "'Course I know, everyone in this town that's got
     a radio
or a television knows. Jesus, lord have mercy, help me
with these nails."

9)
And like this I come to speak before you.
Except I can not talk right
on account of the jaw still being wired
and because I don't know hardly
what to say anymore. When I hated I knew.
Now I don't know
nothing, except the things I told you.
Love opens you up
worse than a knife.

Impossible

*For Chuck and for the students in our lunchtime drug and
alcohol groups at Oakland High School*

Because they are *guys* first of all,
their long legs restless under desks, huge knees jostling.
The way they ball up dirty napkins and shoot for the basket
    while someone else is talking,

and then they miss, and have to get up, heavily and loudly
in the midst of someone else's sentence.
Their too-big pants sliding down artfully to reveal checkered
    boxer shorts,

their elaborate sneakers pumped-up like low-rider car tires,
their hair twisted into twenty tiny pigtails
in an intricate aboriginal initiation ritual

to the tribe of the street.
Or shaved in elaborate patterns,
or a tight nylon skullcap for that gang member look.

Because they're boys and I'm a woman—
because their bones weigh more than mine,
and the dense muscles packed on their bones

like fans at a wrestling match packed into the bleachers
all cheering and shouting, doing the wave—
because everything in them wants to live

leaping and flying against the fence
of the football stadium of their desires, catching the one
    impossible long pass—
and because everything

in the machine outside wants to crush the life out of them,
because boys exactly like them, their brothers and cousins
    and best friends

are sitting in nine by twelve foot cells, shitting in rusty toilets
 with no seat,

thrown into solitary, beaten and violated routinely —
because all of you know this
and still the hormones in their splendid bodies don't believe
 it, still

the urge to *leap that fence,* and here we sit, talking
in a semi-foreign language
they are gamely trying to translate

being boy-men of goodwill; *keyed* means stoned, it's the key
 that opens
the door to that softer world where colors don't have edges
and everything's funny, what we called weed is *bammer,*
 rhymes with hammer,

it's what you fill a cigar skin with, to become a *blunt:*
instrument of self-defense, or tool to penetrate reality.
We bring in apples, they stuff

them down the hoods of each other's sweatshirts.
We say *life,* and the shine on their faces
tells you it is coursing through them, it's like telling

Life itself to be careful, you fear it is threatened
must it run so fast, so hard, and hearing Life say back
I know I know but I can't help it.

Listening to Helen Caldicott on the Car Radio While Stalled in a Traffic Jam Downtown

I like to drive.
To use electricity, gas, fuel.
To step on a pedal and roar forward,
sixty miles an hour.
I like my car,
from whose confines I view, if not rule,
the world. I like my radio,
which sings me songs and tells me stories
when I turn it on, and here's this shrill

Australian woman
yelling, scolding, haranguing.
"My God!" she is saying.
"The trees are your lungs—can't you see?
They look just like a pair of upside-down lungs.
The rivers and oceans are your arteries,
your blood. The ozone your skin.
Don't you get it?
The earth is not your mother— it is yourself!"

She is screeching
through the unreal fog of traffic.
I inch forward slowly, sweating.
I could turn her off. With one flick of my wrist.
I am that powerful.

I remember
hearing her speak in a huge auditorium filled with people.
"How many of you," she asked, in that steel sandpaper voice
    of hers,

"would die to save the earth?"
Some hands went up.
My husband, sitting beside me, raised his.
I could not.
He was crying.

Still I could not.

Ode to the Jacuzzi at the 23rd St. Y

I'm up to my neck in hot bubbles,
up to my eyeballs in the shared flesh of the mothers
who pad softly across the tiles,
some with a modest and inadequate
white towel knotted under their breasts,
others simply, unashamedly clothed
in the pleasure of their own skin.
We're a menagerie of no mean proportions;
one woman looks like a stork,
skinny, mottled legs
beneath a huge, wobbly behind.
Another is massively elegant,
like a rhino, lowering
herself to the blessing of water.
There are the young Asian girls, dark nipples
like the centers of black-eyed Susans,
their slim waists and the slight
buds of their hipbones like the beginnings
of antlers on yearling deer.
There are two black women,
rosy bronze shoulders, legs like trees,
their hair tied up in strips of marigold
sun-cloth from Kenya.
No such beast as white here;
the heat draws color
to everyone's skin, just different shades
of terra cotta, peach, blood honey. I'm part fish, floating
unanchored, all breath and bubbles in this place
where their bodies are my body, are all our body,
the childbirth scars, the folded breasts,
the innocent long crack bisecting the buttocks,
the dark country of the labia
as one hoists herself up awkwardly
onto the wet tiles and another slips
shyly then surely into the water.

Janus

Why, even when her slender fingers part
the slippery soft lips of me
and sliding enter,
with the strength
of all that desire,
do I miss you
coming into me from behind that way
we had,
do I miss the sweet pain of your entrance,
your hot breath in my ear
whispering *wife, my own
forever wife,*
promising the impossible?

                             Holding

her warm curves I feel how faithful
some part of me stays
to the long muscle of your body
and your satin cock with its one slit
weeping eye.
As one of my eyes
is always weeping
for what's past and gone,
always looking backwards
as well as forwards into time
even as my body learns the new
joys of this love's
melody, her breath, her tears
when she comes, shaking,
clenched around my awed
and radiant fingers.
Still I remember
the smell that would pour
from you only in those moments,
a rare musk, reserved for me
and you, and that third

being we made together, and I have not lost
all the difficult history
you entrusted to me
your eyes huge and dark as a child,
as now she looks at me, intent on the threshold,
and I look back
through these eyes, these speechless worlds.

Susan said what could a man

give her that you couldn't and I said
tiny pointed nipples, smell
of a man, a warm hard cock
moving inside her, hard buttocks under her hands
like an underripe nectarine,
sound of a man moaning in her ear,
furry chest, face full of hair, smell
of a man smells different
from a woman and what she
gives me that a man can't
is softness sloping into hardness
the round mountain ridge of her hip
and then the soft breasts rising, a handful each,
broader flatter nipples that need to be licked
and sucked to a point, woman's breath of wheat and milk,
smell of a woman, rich, and her small turnings over and under
and beside me all the long night, hands in my hair
and the way she tries to stare
into my skull, green eyes vs. brown, man vs. woman,
are you laughing or crying and the answer is of course.
There is no argument because I love both
too, and sometimes neither, but I know
the feeling of being swept up in a man,
bone-crusher, mountain-mover,
and I know the soft vulnerable underneath
parts she loves as well, the way my hand can reach
for his scrotum, hold it close
to the heat of his body, while my other hand
wraps around the long slick
body of his cock and I love how his eyes go
dreamy and faraway in that moment whereas her eyes
could pierce you they are so honest
when we laugh and kiss and interrupt
ourselves, being women, to talk, stop

talking to kiss, interrupt kissing for a talk break, the way the
interruptions are the thing, perhaps the point
of all of it, in a different way than nipples
become pointed, and then her breasts I can go back
and back to them, they fit so well
in my hands.

Swaying Slightly in Geoff's Hammock

The yellow rose smells like peach brandy.
She holds her gold cup to the sun, she shows him
her innermost sex, indelible smudge of burnt-orange pollen,
nothing to hide.
Bud or ripe bloom, leaves rust
on one side, green another,
gray thorns tipped with light.
Even chewed or tattered
a bit by wind and insect there is nothing
that is not perfect. A gray cat
and a black cat stalk each other on the grass,
pretending to be enemies,
and birds drill the air with sound,
intent on their own messages. Each thing is saying
exactly what it means — what is it?
If I were not so stupid
from trying to be good
I would hear
what they know.
As when the fullblown rose petals
begin to curl, brown with lived beauty,
they just drop,
never having known shame.

On Not Flying to Hawaii

I could be the waitress
in this airport restaurant
full of tired cigarette smoke and unseeing tourists.
I could turn into the never-noticed landscape
hanging identically in all the booths
or the customer behind the *Chronicle*
who has been giving advice about stock portfolios for forty years.
I could be his mortal weariness,
his discarded sports section, his smoldering ashtray.
I could be the 70-year-old woman who has never seen Hawaii,
touching her red lipstick and sprayed hair.
I could enter the linen dress
that poofs around her body like a bridesmaid,
or become her gay son
sitting opposite her, stirring another sugar
into his coffee for lack of something true to say.
I could be the reincarnated soul of the composer
of the muzak that plays relentlessly overhead,
or the factory worker who wove this fake Oriental carpet,
or the hushed shoes of the busboy.

But I don't want to be the life of anything in this pitstop.
I want to go to Hawaii, the wet, hot
impossible place in my heart that knows just what it desires.
I want money, I want candy.
I want sweet ukulele music and birds who drop from the sky.
I want to be the volcano who lavishes
her boiling rock soup love on everyone,
and I want to be the lover
of volcanoes, who loves best what burns her as it flows.

II

Fairy Tale

If I had to ride the red horse of my loneliness
restlessly over the earth
for twenty-seven years and a day of looking,
before I found you and brought you back,
half-dead from extravagant hunger,
to live with me;
and if then I could scarcely believe
our good fortune,
but kept dreaming famine, famine
over the land,
and men still wore
the faces of incomplete strangers
and your warm hand slipped sometimes
out of my grasp like water
and I kept turning around to look,
although that was expressly
forbidden,
and if we kept losing each other
all over again and having to pack up and go
back to the country of the dead
or the desert or brave the witch
a third time in her castle of ice, hiding
the stolen tinderbox under our rags...
So what?
Anything was worth it
to bring us both back
to daylight generously inventing geometry on our quilt,
and your sweet sleep
the odor of damp white flowers resting
in the hollow of my neck, in my arms,
precious as first snow winking to the child
who runs out to claim the ordinary diamonds
that are the wealth of the kingdom, forever.

The Justice of the Peace

She tried to warn us,
that serious dark little steam-shovel of a woman
whom we hired for thirty-five dollars to sign the necessary
    certificate.
She arrived like the messenger of bad news,
stoically prepared to deliver her brief,
even if it meant her death,
and trapped us in the bedroom of the borrowed house,
where she tried to forewarn: after a few years,
he will turn into your father, or you will turn him so.
She will become your mother, or you will make her so.
It always happens, she said darkly,
this long-married woman with short black hair, three kids,
and a husband she'd left
watching games on T.V., his feet up
on something soft.
It happens to everyone
she insisted, angry now because Alan was arguing with her.
No, not us, he fought back.
We're different, months at a time we traveled together,
like two legs carrying one body over a mountain. He wouldn't
    give in.
You don't know us, years
we waited to find each other
on opposite banks of a dangerous river;
the bridge we built, the life we've made somehow
camped up high above the roaring water and the black rocks.

While they wrangled I sat
silent in my rustling yellow taffeta and white lace dress,
    terrified
she'd say *No, you can't be married.*
I, the State,
see right through you to your fundamental

loneliness, you will never be wife material,
you are not even woman
and man, but two wild spirits
who put on flesh the way you purchased
these stitched-together clothes.
I fingered the strand of fake pearls around my neck,
grandmother's long-ago gift.
They were the ivory color of old piano keys,
of an old woman's last teeth.
Off-white, the color of disillusionment and failed beginnings.
No safe place to speak
of the fear that gripped me then.
So we surrendered
and went outside, where tall old elms
whispered together in lush July wind,
sun broke through mist
and our guests shifted on folding chairs and fanned themselves.
There my first friend Helen, robed like a Greek goddess, waited,
her bare arms full of chants and blessings,
and behind her a river
of shimmering faces.
Before the final steps
I took Alan's hand.
His heart beat
so hard it moved the pink of his shirt.
Then everything was moving,
a wave crested and crested inside me
and would not break,
but lifted us both on its back.

I'd known pain had a shape and a taste,
gritty and bitter as false pearls
crushed between my teeth; I didn't know
or dare to hope, that love too was solid as soup;

that it could change forms, now a bridge,
now a great white bird,   now this invisible tidal arc.
As we floated out   hand in hand
over the tops of trees
I looked for the beetle-browed
justice of the peace
far below us
her head bowed in resignation, or prayer.

Fireworks

Desire blooms and bursts where it wants
and the goddess is often unfair

but never absent. She rains
blue and white flowers into the lake.

Here comes a furious rose, popping its buttons
petal by petal, in golds we may never touch.

Why is passion so difficult?
You and me, we watch

magic stretch
like a cat behind a cloud

lonely and arrogant, proud
to perform a few new tricks behind the ancient curtains.

Shape-shifter, wearing a dress of green gunpowder
that opens on spangles and lightning:

nothing. The hoarse cry of a bareback dancer
makes smoke explode

in our hearts.
Tell me, is it like this for everyone?

Noise, a flash, pain behind the eyes...
An umbrella of colored stars rains loss.

We stand under it all night long.
A rose falls into the generous water,

and the moon
tugs at her bonds,

wanting to go higher.

Waiting Up

I am waiting up for you, waiting like wood,
for your heavy particular stress on the stairs,
for the metal that fits your key
and the knob that knows
the exact turning warmth of your hand.
Here where you are still coming home, to me,
to our bed, to the touch of this life
and red dawn breaking from gray clouds in the same
window each morning. You've been my life,
I admit it, for as long as I can bear
to sit in the middle of this moment, waiting
for the smell of your wild black hair,
and your eyes, slippery live brown coffee beans,
and your cheek, cold from driving wrapped in fog, over the midnigl
    bridge.
There was a time we fought and screamed in the car and it poured
    deafening sheetfulls of rain.
There was forgiveness, like sudden, unexpected quiet,
after which the rain starts up again, but gentler
like all the stories from my childhood that you have learned by hear
so I could forget them
if I wanted to. So I could rest
a moment and feel the future
carry me along, swift current under our canoe.
The river was real, was no dream.
I still remember showing you the place where lady-slippers
hid themselves in the Northern woods,
and how often you crossed
over the slippery falls to bring me back
something I needed. There is that to keep,
and the rest to let go.
There was a long conversation
I thought we'd finish
differently. There were nightbirds crying.
There was the whole dream, unbroken in the water.
There is still the water, there is always the water.

44

Like Ruth in the Alien Corn

I feel my way through the tall rustling cornfield.
The blind silk ears finger my hair
and dry stalks slash my face.
I walk into the alien corn
like Ruth, not knowing where I am going
or why I came—or why I stay—
except for the sibilant voice of the serpent
which whispers "Whither thou goest..."
What kind of crap is that?
A flock of crows
explodes suddenly, out of nowhere,
out of the corn. You aren't dead
but lost to me. Lost or hiding?
I'm no heroine, just a wife
who's not even sure she's a wife anymore,
stepping gingerly over something the cat caught;
bits of fur, glimpse of bone.
I hunt the empty labyrinth.
Did I leave home, friends, family for this?
I was lost there too, it is not so different.
        —But there was hope then.
Then, a perfect circle, magic ring. Something
which has now slipped from my hand. If it was mine,
how could I lose it? Hunting
will never bring it back again,
yet I keep searching, part leaves
with my body, knee my way around
fat scratchy roots as if I were in the midst of the jungle.
Here, there is only my heartbeat, too loud,
sweat and dirt-streaks, rough smell of sky and corn.
Not one other woman for company.
Who suffers in marriage suffers alone.
And the crop itself is going,
past its time. A few shriveled teeth. Husks.
And it is late

afternoon, late summer, too late
perhaps, though I still
love you and the way
through could be
that close...the sky, my God, is huge.
A mauve sea where clouds on fire shipwreck.
I would like to sail up into it and swim through that fire,
through a black snowfall of exploding crow-feathers.

Monologue for Two Voices

I will stand here in my worst disguise,
plastered with shit and chicken feathers,
blood smeared on my fur and my red eyes rolling like a lunatic
roaring and howling until you love me.
But I can't love you
until you take off that mask that looks like a smashed Cadillac
with roadkill still decorating its damaged and bent front fenders
so that I can see your dear face again—that face
whose lines and curves I have memorized
like the valley where I want to live out my days.
I can't take off this mask
by myself. Its rusted metal has become part of me, encrusted
    badge
of what we have been through together, so you must love it
the way you loved that sweet trickling stream
that became the raging ocean
that taught you swimming is for surface creatures.
Our type's talent is for drowning. And I will scream here
until you tell me over and over again
that you love me. Until I can hear you.
But I can't hear myself think
or find my voice, the voice I need to tell you I love you
while you are screaming at me that way.
I am nailing my feet to this piece of earth
and I will never move from this spot, or allow you to move
until you promise to marry me,
just as I am.
But how can we marry, what place on earth can we live
with your feet nailed to the ground like that?
Then I will die, alone, howling in the wilderness
for you, lady, a rose crushed between my lips and tongue.
But how can we love, if you are dead,
and what can I do with this bloody rose?

Accidents

In the midst of stop-and-go
self-pity, I steer the car unsteadily;
in another universe, I may have been killed already,
there were that many stop signs rolled through
without looking,
there were all those dark and careless
corners I crossed.
                    In this other universe
collapsed in its black
suitcase like an unprovable
law of physics, we haven't met yet,
and I am still surprised
when you hand yourself to me, strange as a winter rose,
and I grasp hold,
eager and uncomprehending,
glad even when the unexpected
thorns tattoo my hand.
Although in the ninth
or tenth dimension I marry perhaps
some nice, ordinary man,
and raise wide-eyed children;
although in another one still
I go to Africa as planned,
ride all night on the leopard of my anger
and return a shaman, or never return at all;
although I am dead already,
although I am not yet born,
although the children I might have had
are doing the cakewalk,
the rhumba, the cha-cha-cha somewhere immaterial—
in this world where I married you, I would do it again,
not resisting the dangerous
flower with its painful strange fragrance
of rust and garlic and another person's tears mingled with mine,
the aching-sweet crushed-petal smell of love

still pungent even after
it has left the room.
Even knowing what I know.
Even here, in this ridiculously
difficult world where traffic doesn't stop
for a woman crying in her car,
clutching the steering wheel hard with both hands.

Monogamy

She's practicing again.
My next-door neighbor,
a dark-haired woman, who lives as I do, alone,
is doing scales on her oboe—
lovely word: *ovum, bone, abode* – over and over.
Her practice repeats like conversation
between a long-married couple,
who speak in grunts and sighs: *mmm-hmm*:
Work. Family. Money.
The same worries and desires as yesterday.
The same pleasure in speaking them.
My cat stops scratching in his box to listen.
Every night she does this, my neighbor,
she makes a staircase of sound
on which my loneliness floats far out
and faithfully returns.
                                    So that cooking,
or washing, or paying bills
at the kitchen table, I listen for her,
grateful to lean into the pure
building of song—*sob, long* – she erects
against night's foreclosing.

And I want to be faithful—*free-fall; fierce, thirsty, wakeful* —
to something,
now that there is nothing, any longer, to cling to.
The marriage is gone. Only some papers
to sign and we are free
to be strangers. I remember
coming home to you once
after a discussion, with friends,
about non-monogamy. In bed,
deliciously, comfortably
naked, next to your warm back,
I asked what you thought of it

and you replied, *I prefer poly-wogamy.*
Which seemed, in that moment,
like the sweetest response anyone could give—
honoring by not insisting on
that charged word,
which sounds to me now
like a long sad cello note, like a cow
lowing for her babe, like nothing
I can own or know.

The Notary Public

to whom I bring the last bits of our marriage, written on legal sheets
has hair dyed the color of an Easter chick, and stabbing-black masca
Her eyes are green and tired. She can't resist
looking over her bifocals and asking, "Is it amicable?"
I've just handed her the letter from the man who called himself my
    husband
listing the division of our property.
"Sort of," I say, not that it's any of her business.
"I don't want a divorce," I confess.
She looks sharp. "Why then?" "It's a long story."

She leafs through the document, the size of a skimpy novella,
reads me the paragraph I have to agree to, asks me to raise my right
    hand.
I can't. I don't agree. I would have rather died than come to this pla
I think if Alan and I were chained together
in a small room and made to work it out, we could.
And I think no one else can ever know,
not his lawyer, not this notary, no judge, no family or even friends
who didn't taste the sweetness between us,
not even ourselves, who were there,
can fathom, completely,
what we lost when we lost each other.

I can't raise my right hand, can't answer her.
She lowers her glasses, looks at me sternly. "It's over, you know."
Then proceeds to tell the story of her sister's husband
who wanted to stay married though he'd fathered a child
with a *Japanese* woman — "Can you believe it?
I told him God was punishing him,
giving him a Japanese son to go with his two blond half-sisters."
"I think God blessed him with a child."

We exchange a glare
of bitterness and understanding, then move on,

through grief's deepest sinkholes back to life
with its unwinnable arguments.
I realize she has been trying to help me,
however clumsily, through the gates of hell.
I swear where I have to. I sign.
Then she tells about her husband,
disabled fourteen years, whom she supports
and visits weekly in a Veteran's Hospital.
"It's not what I expected from life. When he dies
I won't marry again. No,
I've had it. I'll take my freedom."
"Do you love him?" She frowns.
"Sure I love him. What's that got to do with it?"
Okay, so her pain too, goes down to the core of the earth.

I fold up my papers to go. She looks at me
as if we've just been through a ritual together
which we have, and says, "I wish you the very best."
"Yes, and to you also."
And we almost bow to each other,
as if we were Japanese people,
schooled in the crucial art of ceremony.

Dear Michael,

I wish you could see our squash plant,

how she's snaked a long green runner across the yard, sprawling
onto the patio, flouting her yellow flowers,
trumpeting triumphant surrender
to the life force that's forcing her to take over the world.

Of course, we planted everything
too close together,
the dill went to seed, cherry tomatoes are crowded
so densely you can hardly get an arm in to weed or pick,

and the red-faced Israeli sunflowers got too tall and fell over.

And I'm the same, you know me
I want everything and the nothing it birthed out of,
knowing I can't have *anything*
unless I surrender attachments as we discussed —

which is tricky, somewhat akin
to hiding the chocolate chips from yourself
because you're on a diet, meanwhile
only you know where those chips are hidden — I know you know

what I mean: why would desire be planted so fiercely in us if not for
    some good reason?

When everywhere you look the plants are screaming to grow
and give, and bear, even if they break themselves
in the process, they don't care
about that, the other leg of the squash reaches out to the compost hea

and the peach trees I wrote you about that I was afraid
were too spindly to produce have shot up two feet in my absence
and are dropping perfumed fruit
at our feet and into our open hands.

The Largest Possible Life

for Ruth and Gladys

Building a fire, love;
  bent low
    over a flame

I am afraid of.
  Coaxing passion
    from dry twigs

and dead leaves,
  the failures of the past, dirty fingers,
    and a moment of sunset

huge orange
  hangs in one eye—
    in my breast a sun

which, if I could see it, if I could
  know it, would
    light the world

with love. Then,
  an unexpected memory
    of my mother in the car, snow piled

along the gray streets
  of Massachusetts. It was my sixteenth year
    and we were fighting a life

and death struggle over my desire to give
  myself away completely to love before
    I had a self to give.

There she was, my block, my barricade,
  my iron grate, my broken door—our one shared
    passion, to hurt each other into truth, and

it was the millionth skirmish
    of our everyday war when she said
        "I don't know if I've ever loved anyone,"

and began to weep. Monks sit
    in the middle of fires
        they set themselves. They let

their bodies bloom
    into suffering,
        in the hope that, like this, they will open

someone's heart.
    What do we have to
        see, how close do we need to live by the

beautiful terrible flame of this world,
    flame of ourselves, which is
        the same thing?

How much anguish do we need to pour
    from cup to cup, drink of melted rubies,
        underwater food of the fevers that live

in our blood, in the light of our eyes
    where infinite tears are waiting and still
        you say, "Light a white candle," and I do, asking

whoever it is, *Teach me to surrender*
    this mind that grasps at shadows
        when the whole house is ablaze, when the only thing left

is to leap, carrying the impossible
    weight in my arms, into
        the heart of our fire, to melt and to bloom.

Jesus Incognito

Don't tell anyone, but I love Jesus.
I love his big dark Jewish eyes, so full of suffering soul,
like an unemployed poet, and his thick sensuous Jewish lips,
and his kinky curly hair, just like mine, uncontrollable despite
    conditioners,
and the way he always argues with everyone
and will go to Hell for love.
He's just like that Buddhist god Avalokiteshvara, the
    emanation of compassion,
except his name is easier to pronounce.
When you're in trouble it's hard to remember to yell for
    Avalokiteshvara,
but "Oh Jesus!" arises naturally
every time a crazy driver hot-dogs past me on the freeway.
I know I should say the Shema when I'm about to die,
but will I be able to remember Hebrew at the right time?
I don't want to die saying "Oh shit!"
I'd like to leave my body consciously like a Tibetan lama,
sitting in full lotus, with my head turned towards where I'll
    reincarnate next.
But let's be realistic: I probably don't have time to meditate
    enough to get enlightened
in the however many years I have left.
Jesus seems easier. All you have to do is love everyone.
Well, *seems* is the key word here.
Sometimes the more you try
to love people, the more you hate them.
Maybe it would be better to try
not to love people, and then watch the love
force its way out of you like grass through cement, etc.
Anything is better than organized religion.
Plus, I don't like the singing in churches—those hymns in
    major keys.
I don't think religion should sound so triumphant.
It should be humble and aware of the basic incurable pathos
    of the human condition

and in a minor key and sung in an ancient mysterious
     language, like Sanskrit or Hebrew.
Is it okay if I want to love Jesus but not be Christian?
I could just try to open my heart and give away my
     possessions.
It's not that different from being Buddhist after all, except for
     a history
of witch-burnings, the Inquisition, subjugation,
rape and pillage of indigenous peoples all over the world,
not to mention twenty centuries of vicious anti-Semitism.
     That's a lot to overlook
to get back to a baby born among animals to a Jewish mother,
     Miriam.
And that other Mary, the sexy one. Jesus, I don't believe you
     died a virgin.
I think you needed to taste everything human, inhabit the
     whole mess:
blood, shit, flies, regret, envy, why-me—
I owe you and all the other bodhisattvas and sages
and new-born babies a debt of thanks
for agreeing to come back and marry yourselves
to our painful predicament again and again—
and I do thank you, bowing to the infinite directions.

Stripping

Strip off the shoes and pantyhose,
the grown-up drag. Undo

those soft white arms and their blonde down,
moss made of light.

Wash away the sour sweat,
fatigue of heels and fluorescent lights.

Unhook that tired bra, release the feet
with their worn-out travelogues,

knees, complaining in their bone cradles,
the drooling sex, and the shamed

belly, pouched like a stubborn mountain.
Release the years in a shower of moths shaken free

from an old sweater, so full of holes
you can see through to the skin.

Strip off the skin. Let it hang
over a chair the way it has hung

from your body lately, exhausted,
confessing to years of experience.

Strip away experience, that false umbrella
blocking the only sun.

Strip your mind of these words, clods
of dirt kicked up by donkey mind, clouds

that will soon pass. Let the clang of language die
in your mouth. Let your overworked tongue

hang, innocent and dumb
as tomorrow morning. No one owns it yet,

that paper mini-dress of time, meant
to be cast off after one wearing.

It's the jewel at the center
I seek; let me be oyster, hoarding pearl,

let me be coal, sheltering diamond.
Though in my heart of hearts I fear

I may be onion, each white circle
of stinky tears hiding another

exactly like it. Or rose:
whose petals *are* her everything.

Bad Date

Trying to talk with this man is like trying to drive through a
      blizzard.
My hands grip the steering wheel grimly.
My eyes are searchlights, peering through permafrost,
looking for a road somewhere out of the storm of his words.
The wheels keep slipping, threatening to strand us
      somewhere in the middle of a drift,
I can't see two feet in front of his argument,
I don't even know what he's arguing about, now he seems to
      be smiling
as if he thought I agreed with him—
Don't panic!

Times like these, I miss my ex-husband.
I miss every man I ever had a reasonable conversation with.
I miss silence.

Being alone with this guy's thoughts
is like being on a squash court
with that vicious little ball bouncing off
the walls floor ceiling everywhere.

The waitress in the beautiful sari
has refilled our water glasses three times
but he doesn't feel he should leave a tip
because they didn't display their sign boldly enough outside.
He walked past three times, looking for the place.
He has asked to speak to the manager.

What's it like to be this guy?
Be in his head, I mean.
Talking to him, I feel like a frozen mouse,
about to be fed to a child's pet snake.
We have discussed my work and his work and agreed we

both do Important Things.
We have talked about yoga, and meditation, and politics, and, god
    help us, therapy.
First thing tomorrow, I will run away and join the circus.

Will I ever be with a man again like water braiding itself with water,
unconcerned as it whispers against wet stones?
Will it ever be that dance again, simple and mysterious as laughter
arising from nowhere, arising from the belly in wordless warm
    waves?

Now he has taken a deep breath and looked moistly into my eyes.
I think that means I am responsible for his emotional well-being.
He is getting ready to recite
one of his poems. Maybe there will be an earthquake
and the chandelier will fall on our heads and I'll be spared.
Maybe a madman
will come in brandishing a gun and hold up this restaurant,
And I'll scream "Guido! What took you so long?" and launch
    myself into his arms,
and the getaway car will be parked outside, idling.

Valentine's Day in the 8th Grade

Outside, the rhythmic thump of basketballs on asphalt
and yelling and screaming from gym class.
Inside, the kids lean over their ragged scraps of paper,
writing a word, crossing it out, writing it over again.

Lining up, the rows of 8th grade boys push each other into lockers
to express the love that dare not say its name.
The girls are writing volumes. They favor light green ink, or purple.
The popular ones have gifts of teddy bears on the corners of their
    desks,

or a single rose, wrapped with a twist of babies' breath,
sheathed chastely in plastic.
The air is red with the beauty of their lips pursed in thought,
or hung half-open in the slackness of desire.

Pain hums a half-note below Romance
who is stalking the room with her bow and arrows, looking for easy
    prey.
She finds it, sure, but not so many as Heartbreak
who has already drawn a net around the quieter ones.

I measure my own strength
against the weight of the questions I carry
and find the questions heavier than ever this year,
although my heart is wider.

Oh, Love, my arms are tired.
I would like to set you down, on a scarred desk,
gently, in front of one of the younger ones.
They still know everything.

Instead, I walk up and down between rows
chanting my grocery list of ideas.

"Where does Loneliness live? What does Truth wear?
Who does Love like to hang around with?"

And Tony J., who up till now has shown a genius
only for making farting noises with his hand and asking
     questions like
"Mr. Messler, how do you spell 'puke'?" says "Love?
That's easy. Love will hang out with anyone."

Moss Landing

We are paddling into the slough,
past plumes of factory smoke and the buzz of agri-business on 101.
Just far enough to get away from human noise,
gliding by guano-stained rocks where a convention of herons
stares straight ahead, then rises,
with one mind, into early morning fog and disperses.
We are dipping our oars
as quietly as wooden stirrers in dawn coffee.
When you can't hear the freeway anymore,
you can see the seals
popping up like periscopes, a black rubber bathing cap,
eyes intelligent as a dog's
and three slits for nostrils. It is so quiet we can hear them breathe,
hoarsely, like a child with a cold, *sjhaa, sjhaa.*
We can let our paddles rest idle.
The current is taking us.

It's easy to forget how to be alive,
and then on such mornings it all comes back to us, simply:
feel your body beloved inside the cradle of the canoe,
rocking gently through cold water,
last night's lovemaking warm inside your pants,
pooling a little, the way a small puddle of bay water
forms under you, dipped from the paddles.
Fog wrapped softly like a gauze bandage
around everything you can't control: water's swiftness,
or the way this last year has flown
like a night whose dreams you can't remember.
A run of ripples means we have to get back before the tide turns.
And the tide is turning fast,
old lover. More time behind than ahead
for us. But then the open sea.

The Last Time We Made Love

We didn't know it was the last time.
It felt like all the other times,
a little bit different of course, each time is.
You traced under my clavicle with hard thumbs pressing deep
into my green-veined breasts, the way God
spent eons furrowing riverbeds through the clay of mountains.
Pushing with the fever of flesh wanting to know, finally,
what else it is made of,
all the while pouring blue light
from your Puritan-preacher-innocent-boy-trapped-in-hell-
eyes into mine. Eyes through which your father and grandfather
and great-grandfather, towering shadows,
breathed again and looked in wonder
as I screamed and came, three, four, five times,
your fingers hooked into me now,
burning an insistent electrical wave,
my long legs slung over your lion shoulders
so we could admire together the musculature
of what we were making: love, a swaying bridge
of joined bodies, one man, one woman, old, young,
pushed and thrusting in that ancient rhythm, through time
until there was none left; still, we used it well, didn't we?

Choosing It

At the hour of my conception
a taxi was idling in front of an airport
awaiting the passenger with her carry-on luggage.
In the airport bar a waitress
tiredly wiped down tables after the evening shift:
water glass rings, full ashtrays.
January, and the last Canada geese escaping toward the tropics,
honking and crying, their necks extended into the future air.

It was ten years after the last big war.
Men who had liberated concentration camps
were home now, with their nightmares and shiny new cars.
My mother took off her apron,
her dress, unfastened her garter belt with its rubbery snaps.
My father finished brushing his teeth, his pajamas loose on his
    lanky boy frame.
Younger than I am now,
or have ever been, impossibly young,
the world being younger, despite what had been recently learned
about human horror, still—the innocence of them.

I hovered at the window, an unclothed soul,
my breath a fog of invisible ice.
Angels around me cried in their high voices,
"Oh child, don't go!
You will enter in fear and depart in agony,
all the while subject to unendurable longing.
Worms will nibble your brightness,
the tigers of loneliness tear you open,
minnows of trivia devour your days with worry.
Your heart will be a drum of fate, beating senselessly, out of
    control...
your heart, oh! think
how it will hurt you."
                And I said,
"Worms? Minnows? Tigers? Music?"
And dove through the darkened pane
just as her hand reached out to draw the curtains.

At the Ice Rink

for Ruth and Hilary

I came here to fail
and to fall
but not so well
as that man careening over the ice
sliding into the wall as if into second base
shambling up, grinning, like a great bear,
and taking off again,

saying, over his shoulder,
"You've got it backwards.
Learn to fall first,
then skate."

I end up clinging
barnacle-like to the sides,
inching around the perimeter like a caterpillar.
Wall-hugger. Nothing has changed since I was eight
and my parents paid for skating lessons
in hopes I would become more balanced.

Now as then I am wobbling, terrified,
feet frozen like blocks of wood at the ankles.
Not loose-limbed and easy like Hilary
who rides the ice like a North wind scouring the plains,
nor deft and graceful like Ruth
picking up her feet and kick-gliding
in time to the 70's pop muzak.

But what can we do
when fear throws its rustiest pickaxe
dead ahead in our path?

Mince. Inch. Stumble. Pray
for the grace to fall

and not be rescued, pray for the scramble-up,
for the liberating laughter that knows

it is not in our control.
There is the center, gleaming like a fish-eye.
Little girls spin on it, twirling their bright skirts.
It shines under its white scars like a destiny.

III

Outdoor Wedding

for Emily and David

The young uncorked wine is waiting
for someone to say yes
and start pouring. The sky
is green with summer rain.

A dark horse rides up with a bride on its back,
my sister. Slender and nervous.
Her white dress drifts backwards.

They advance toward the canopy
where we hold the rain in our arms,
a great hope
for the future.

The bride bursts into tears,
then the groom,
then everyone.

I watch my mother in her wheelchair,
my father's hand on her shoulder,
both of them leaning forward eagerly
like children.

The first grandchild has wriggled
out of his mother's arms
like a fat fish and run down
to drop stones in the pond:
plunk! plunk!

We stand together under this canopy
in the green rain
with the shivering frogs
the trees full of aged light,

the four-leggeds and the eight-leggeds
paused in their serious mating;

God watches us through the eyes of birds,
through the hiding fish,
through the rain caught in the throats of flowers,
through anything.

Vigil

One sister is knitting
a mass of gray snakes on her lap.
It will become a vest

someday.
The other watches;
their mother is dying

between them,
or trying to.
The ill-fitting

oxygen mask
keeps slipping off her face
like a giant pacifier

falling out as the baby nods off.

Her harsh breathing
measures
the ordinary peace of the room.

The sisters resist the longing to fall asleep
through the slenderest part of the night
when a life could pass,

like a swaybacked camel
over the farthest hump of the mountains,
and get lost there

among all the other mountains.

The one who knits
keeps leaning forward
and adjusting the chin strap

beneath the terrifying open mouth—

she is the precise one, who can't help fixing
whatever is there—spilled water pooling
beneath a vase of flowers,

a dying mother—
but with such deft
tenderness, that the other, the watcher,

sees it as prayer. Outside, in the corridor,
nurses wheel and squeak
discreetly, in their white sneakers.

And beyond them, the big outside:
a merciful snow
blurs and blots the landscape, turns day and night

inside-out, the way a woman will reverse
a fuzzy sweater
before washing.

It's a lie. There is no such thing as *outside*.

Meanwhile, the one whose job
it is to notice such things, notices
how her sister's beauty

shines out—
the planes and angles of her young face
passionately attentive,

exhausted, and sad.
It is the same
bright flame, hooded look

that once pierced
their father. Years and years back,
when the body was the bright thing,

gold coin, live prize,
fished from the wishing fountain.
Heart, eyes — where did it go?

This moment. Then the next.
And the terrible breathing
and thrashing for breath continues.

Morning in the Mission; Grandpop Comes to Visit

The fog drifts in like an old man snoring sadness,
licking the wet end of an ancient cigar.
It's my grandfather, dead these thirty years.
I smell his breath rising from the open backs of trucks
where men stand knee-deep in corn, tossing ears into crates.
I taste him in the coffee I buy at the corner,
bitter as an alarm clock, real as dirt.
Slosh a little libation onto the curbstones.
A long-gone taste of what you've been missing, Grandpop.
You came such a far way from Brooklyn, just to visit me.
I've never felt him near me, never tasted his presence
all these years. Dead is dead. So tell me
how it happens that Yinglish becomes Spanglish after the family
has scattered into strange cities and changed names
a few times but still the blood
in my veins sings morning, morning. Our lives are rain
poured into the ocean, rough surf, sweet surf,
and you know souls often skip
down the generations, playing tiddlywinks with Western logic.
So Grandpop rides his old newspaper truck past 24th and Mission
in the early morning chill, as if it were New York in the 50's.
He's still smoking the cheap stogies that killed him,
and he's in his shirtsleeves
though July here will freeze you faster than vanished love.
The dead don't care anymore, about such things.
Only, they like to do a day's work
through us, now and then, when we let them.
And they appreciate the chance to look around,
see how things have changed.

That woman there, biting into a wet plum, I'd like to bury
my face in her lilac cleavage and just inhale.
In my day, ladies didn't wear their underwear on the streets, but who's to say?
I might get used to seeing you in your tights.
The kids are cute as city squirrels, their big eyes shine and you wish —

oh, you don't have anything to wish for
anymore, but if you could hold one of them again,
it would be the world. One day you're gonna to be looking back, like me,
through the eyes of some young person, and everything will seem different.
The grit in your eyes will be gone and streets will shine silver
when light hits them, and you'll see it as jewels
everywhere, even on the battered face of the old guy
with two brown teeth left in his head who mutters gibberish to no one
on the corner of South Van Ness.
You'll hear him swearing, "Hijo de puta! Pendejo!"
and you'll swear it's a prayer
for the living who drive their trucks and take their busses
and jingle loose change in their pockets, like they always did —
the busy ones like you who think,
think, think about everything except this life
here, now, under their feet, a new day wrapped in fog
like a birthday present, its ribbons shining
while you stand preoccupied at the curb
waiting for the everlasting green light.

You have to make a family because you can't

and you have to make it out of broken city;
muddy puddles, slivers of moon.

Make it out of broken because everything is.
You'll have to walk by dark water first, a long time,

and sometimes alone. Around the lake is a good place to start,
because the sweet water ends there and the dark salt sluices in.

In the mud where they mix sleep the ducks
each one with her head, his head

tucked under a wing. In the night the family of everything
clusters together, huddled against the chill wind of nothing.

How can the ducks sleep like that, bobbing and floating on the cold
    dirty water
How can we make family out of ourselves when we are empty

and lonely to boot? A water rat scurries along slick stones,
keeping pace with our wavering shadows, our eager, anxious
    voices.

Being human, we can't figure anything out.
The trees hear us and laugh, their roots touch underground.

They sleep and wake to the splashing of pelicans, the ceaseless tide
    of traffic,
the snoring of the homeless man on a bench alongside.

Dark earth holds them up.

Stolen Sentences for Abraham

Stolen. One dollar. By one small skinny black boy
with sugar smeared on his face,
white sugar speckling the tough curls on top of his head,
and eyebrows like exaggerated question marks —
Who me?
And me, hurt, white grown-up
with lots of dollars to buy mountains of candy,
more than anyone could want — *Yes, you. How could you, Abraham?*
So I kicked him out, barred him from my house FOREVER
and thought to myself *That's what I get for...*
Didn't finish the sentence.

Only later, cleaning up the house, alone,
still throbbing with self-righteousness, I remembered
"Property is theft," Phil always used to say, serenely,
whenever I bumped someone else's car, trying to park, and didn't
    leave a note,
or scratched the floor of a rented apartment.
Sometimes, as a young person, I stole — a pair of pants
I just wanted once, they were too expensive,
so I wore them out of the dressing room, under my own baggy
    jeans,
under the nose of the security guard.
I've stolen Tampax when I was mad at the patriarchy.
I've certainly tried to avoid paying taxes, I've stolen time
at work to make personal phone calls, write these poems — doesn't
    everyone do it?
We learn early and harshly:
this is mine, that's yours.
And then go through life, taking and taking
trying not to get caught.
And one young boy in front of my house,
his people long ago stolen from their homeland and brought here,
labor stolen, language lost, children taken

81

from their mothers and sold—he's kicking pebbles, "on
    punishment" already
for throwing a rock that hit his sister in the eye—
though he says he didn't mean it—asking me,
"Patty can come in but I can't? Why?"
"You know why."
"Cause I stole?"
"Yeah, and it made me mad."
Elementary lessons. Abraham, I am late myself, in unlearning
    separation.
Just what the hell do I think I'm trying to teach you now,
and what *am* I teaching you, small, outlawed
piece of my heart out there, scuffing your lonely
bottle-cap and insisting you didn't do it, didn't do it, didn't do it?

Tall Tale for Roy

Our neighborhood's trashed
and blooming. It's the kids,
hellbent on rollerblades,
on beat-up bikes, taped-together skateboards,
whatever wheels they can get ahold of,
who whoop and swoop and make it live.
Kids hanging off the scraggly fig trees,
throwing green fruit, teasing dogs.
Kids on the stoop. Almost like anyone else's old times.
And my neighbors,
ancient bent-over ladies in slippers and turbans,
who step carefully on Sundays on their way to church,
grow persistent roses and call everyone "baby."
They watch over us.

I took Roy, age six,
to check out redworms in the community garden.
He likes how they curl naked in his small palm,
seeking the shelter of dirt.
Lowly miracle-workers, earth-poopers and makers.
The blue sky was rich enough to eat
and lick the bowl afterwards.
Sun like dry champagne.
Roy wanted to water everything in sight.
Little boy, big hose.
Here and there. The lettuces, the beans
unfurling. "There you go, the plants are all saying,
'Thanks for the water, Roy, we were thirsty!'"
He looks up, astonished.
"How they know my name?"

How many boys on my block
will beat the fatherless odds to grow up?

Then and there I know, no question, what I want.
I want this one, avid-eyed, full of tall tales

of all the bad guys he can whup;
this busy brain behind this particular round forehead with
    the keloid scar,
whose mother's a crack addict,
whose big brother's already hard as a hubcap, broken-off—
I want him to live to be a man.
And no half-measures either.
I want him to become the kind of man who will
water things that grow. And to know
always, that someone calls his name.

Saga of the Seven League Pogo Sticks

I cruise Toys R Us, a non-parent in dark sunglasses,
frantic for presents for the neighbor kids.
Christmas is almost upon us, godammit,
and I need what can't be bought.

Fluorescent lights bounce off plastic window boxes
behind which Barbie reclines, pink princess receiver in hand,
having conference call phone sex
with Ken and Skipper and all the Power Rangers.
I prowl like a bear trapped in a shopping mall,
crashing over boxes in my lonely panic: *Not this. Not this.*

Patty says she wants a Barbie
but which kind? One with a convertible.
Okay, my gap-toothed, rollerblading, eight-year-old princess,
shiny Nefertiti extensions braided heavy on your neck—
here we go. Fasten your seatbelt.

When you love a child, you return with her
to the place you swore you would never return,
naked and alone. I'm so unfit for this!
Like a runaway Slinky, a florid Hula-Hoop.
But that was my childhood: lonely, suburban, quaint.
Hers is MTV, gunshots popping outside our frightened windows,
talks-to-himself man lurching behind his shopping cart.

Is this what makes me want
pogo sticks for every child in the neighborhood?
So they can vault over the broken pavement
in front of the crack-houses, over the dying
rose-bushes and parched lawns filled with trash?

There was a reason
I never had kids of my own.
What am I doing here,

lurking among the nerf balls and the stuffed giraffes?

And what is it in my life now
I want to jump over,
never looking down, never looking back?

City Beach

It's summer! The air's unbreathable. The children yearn for
    the mythical ocean.
They ask, *Does it cost money?*

and, *Will there be other kids there?*
On the drive over, Abraham, out of the blue,

says, *Ali, who invented the word* car?
I bet he rich now, huh.

Bet you can make a million dollars
thinking up a word like that.

Last night on the freeway I was startled by the full moon
as it rose, low on the horizon, bulging with gravity,

golden, through the purple smog of Eastbound traffic.
Now I have these children

from the other side of not-mine—Patty lies down
immediately, full-length, luxuriating,

then digs herself a shallow cradle,
like a turtle about to lay her eggs,

and I can see her as a turtle, see
how many centuries she's labored

through a foster childhood in West Oakland, at the end of the
    twentieth century.
Her new breasts bud through her old bathing suit.

We've brought an umbrella, chicken salad, Cheeze-its, a bag
    of cherries.
Sunblock for me. We set up camp, and they scamper

down to the dubiously tea-colored water.
I decide not to think about dioxin

in the bay. Instead we have bright green seaweed
to play with, swirling our thighs like the newest color of latex.

And the brother and sister the children find immediately,
the first kids they see will do, what they want is to play.

The girl says to Patty, *Look!*
It's a mermaid necklace,

and drapes her with a string of seaweed.
The boys paddle out on a styrofoam surfboard.

The other kids are white and look well-cared-for.
New bathing suits, surfboards, orthodontia, and someday college.

Their mother and I nod to each other warily.
Now it's who can hold their breath longest

underwater. The children bob in and out of both worlds.
They swim to me. I make like a pier,

hold fast.

Child and Wrinkles

I tell her not to do it, she does it anyway. I tell her it will make me sad and angry, and she wants to know, What will you look like when you are sad and angry? I will have wrinkles, splitting and seaming my forehead like the pleated sand-flats at low tide. I will be wrinkled like an old piece of yellow cloth, thin, frayed, threadbare in places. That's what you will have done to me, you and your brother. Worn me raw and now I've wrinkled, a straight line going up my forehead, splitting my life in two, the part before you were here, when I was one person, and the part after you have gone when I will be beautiful again, like a deserted beach under the full moon.

In my neighborhood now

jasmine hangs over the fence
like a gang of beautiful girls looking for trouble.
There's guys doing figure 8s in the middle of the street,
spinning round and round, loco,
in their souped-up low-riders with huge wheels,
laying rubber you can smell for half a block,
a cloud of stinking machismo.

Ruth and I go to a nice neighborhood, in the Berkeley hills, to wal
and I tell her, I could have had it.
I could have had this view of the bay,
dogwood trees in bloom, deer nibbling the garden.
I'm not bragging, not ashamed. It's just a story I played a part in.
Alan and I were looking at houses,
back when we were married, and he made good money,
and an indefatigable blonde lady realtor in a silver Mercedes
drove us around winding hills enchanted with red maple and
    flowering cherry.
I watched young mothers wheeling their expensive babies
and tried to imagine myself one of them. And failed.

I was afraid I would go crazy, be found out for the fraud I was,
for the way my life is a vacant lot, lonely and various with weeds,
a magnet for hummingbirds and loiterers.
Letters to the editor go on about urban blight,
but me, I need these abandoned cars, I need my neighbors' wash
    strung on a line.

Without weeds, these widows' weeds
I have been wearing the last four years, I would have destroyed
    myself.
I need the shadow behind all this loveliness,
the city it was built to rise above.
Not to be separate, even from sweat and stink and noise—
I need my body like I need the moon,

its ragged loneliness rising in my own chest, lovely
through a haze of pollution or tears.

Oh Ruth, we think we have choices. We have souls
which yearn for the opposite of what we think.
We are not married
or unmarried women, or men, rich or poor, we are fire
raging in the water,
falling gladly into the arms of night.

Interlude

At the heart of all our ponderous work
is a loud silence. Some stillness
in the midst of the busy. As when
the teacher says,
Now write for fifteen minutes,
and the class falls to, bent
over their notebooks — you can hear
the scritch-scratch of pens, a last whispered
flirt or giggle, the jiggle
of butts against seats, and far away,
the sigh of cars on the freeway.

If you listen, you can hear
the pregnant woman dully sucking ice
halfway through a twenty-hour labor.
You can hear the guy on the stalled power motor
breathe a moment before cursing and wiping his face.

In the end, all our striving
comes to nothing. You knew that
already. And in the middle. You knew that too.

The secretary, lulled into trance by the screen saver's hum,
gazes out the window, twisting her earring,
and forgets for a moment all the details
of her upcoming wedding,
forgets even the name of her fiancé.

All our lives
we hear the roar of that silence
and we thrash against it
as the baby in the womb thrashes
toward the waiting nipple and the enormous light.

Full Moon

The men on Alameda Beach
are pulling striped bass from the glittering water.
Small red stars of cigarettes between their fingers.
Poles stationed like sentinels, stuck in the sand,
lines cast far out,
buckets at the ready.
Waves wash over the tired shoreline
like a lace slip over bare brown shoulders.
The men grin to each other, don't say much.
Fish flop in the pail. Sand dabs. Bass.
The bay is full of dioxin; do they know?
They are fishing to feed their families
in a school of different languages: Tagalog,
Hmong, Mien, Spanish, Vietnamese.
In the dark, a man can be a man
or a shadow in the moonlight, voice out of night,
just another kind of animal with two fine, flexible hands.
Each one standing full of private thoughts,
up to his knees in alive water.
Fish know the truth of depth and shimmer,
then the hook and the fatal sparkling air.
The men know what they know
even if tomorrow at the factory, and the next day, and the next,
will press the memory of this freedom
flatter than a glint of mica. Still, it shines.

The Night Crawlers

Must be caught in the dark, coming on to the azaleas.
Must be pulled like a long
tube of snotty life, and placed
in plastic cups for tomorrow's fishing trip.
Must be alive in your hand, writhing
to get *back there.*
Must know what is happening.

Something that seems made of earth itself, but alive like us—
but can't be, wouldn't be
thought of in the same sentence, purely a wriggling verb
not subject, dangling modifier
to what is left unsaid.
Something that will kiss us,
ten, twenty, fifty years from now,
with blind, curious, penis-colored noses.
Will nest in the sack of our former skin,
and delicately, with no special hurry,
disassemble our remembered features
until we can hear the fish we have eaten tomorrow
and the lettuce we tore and chewed tonight
cry out to us from their changing elements
about the world inside the world
inside our pounding wrists.
It hurts to know. It hurts
not to know. Blessed be
the bright hook that delivers us
from the river to the river.

Everything at its core is pure

if only we can get there.
The cops, the glass-littered street
after the accident,

yesterday's paper and the guy
walking his pit bull while talking on his cell phone
are pure.

The dogshit he picks up with a plastic baggie,
and the stained and broken-hearted sidewalk
where skinny trees with no names are struggling through
     asphalt,

are pure, pure, pure,
deep at the core where molecules dance,
clasping each other in creation's crazy waltz.

They are just what they are

and I am just what I am,
stomach growling,
blue sky sailing slowly through my brain,

my moon heart waxing and waning.

The dream I had and didn't remember is pure.
My mixed motives were always pure.
I wanted love

and freedom. I wanted to hide,
to be seen, to embrace, to die
and be reincarnated as a midwife living in a small town,

or a trapeze artist in sequins travelling from circus to circus.

It was always pure desire

especially when just out of reach.
At my core I longed only to touch

essence,
and I came so close!
God knows it was pure

criminal hunger that drove me through my days
and pure thirst that woke me at 3 a.m., tidal confusion aroused,
a wail of police sirens screeching through my heart's back alleys,

pure meat, pure light, a cry lodged in the deep red cavern of my
    throat.